Who do You Say that I Am?

Church Times Study Guide

Who do You Say that I Am?

Exploring our images of Jesus

Jane Williams

CANTERBURY
PRESS
Norwich

© Jane Williams 2005

First published in 2005 by the Canterbury Press Norwich
(a publishing imprint of Hymns Ancient &
Modern Limited, a registered charity)
St Mary's Works, St Mary's Plain,
Norwich, Norfolk, NR3 3BH

www.scm-canterburypress.co.uk

Reprinted 2006

British Library Cataloguing in Publication data

A catalogue record for this book is available
from the British Library

ISBN 1-85311-660-2
978-185311-660-5

Typeset by Regent Typesetting, London
Printed and bound in Great Britain by Gallpen Colour Print,
Norwich 01603 624893

Contents

Introduction

Describing Jesus

Christians are Jesus-people. For us, Jesus is the key to the world. But that doesn't mean that we all agree about how he and his work are best described. 'WWJD' – 'What would Jesus do?' – tends to produce answers as varied as the people asking the question.

Faith in Jesus has driven people to martyrdom, to crusades, to the struggle to abolish slavery, to work among lepers or sit in the House of Lords. Service to Jesus apparently requires some to abandon themselves to poverty, chastity and obedience, and others to rule countries in his name.

We believe that Jesus shows us and teaches us what God is like and how we should live in God's world. We also believe that through his life, death and resurrection, Jesus does for us whatever it is that needs to be done so that we can come back to God as his people. But the minute we try to spell that out in actions and words, we find we have said or done something that some other Christian may find offensive. The trouble is that Jesus matters too much for us to speak lightly about him. Every age and every individual Christian has attempted to describe Jesus and to explain why he matters so much. Multi-volume tomes written by theologians and philosophers, and emotion-filled prayers of believers of every race, are equally making claims about who Jesus is and what he does for us. And that is without starting on the music, poetry and art that he has inspired. Every single one of these attempts at description also tells us a lot about the longings and fears of the people who make them. They tell us what we imagine God to be like, what we think we are here for, what we feel trapped by and in need of rescuing from, what we believe goodness and evil are, how we should relate to each other and how we actually do, the list is endless.

Being and doing

You might think that it is easier to answer the question 'who is Jesus?' than 'what does he do for us?' and, traditionally, theology has divided discussion about Jesus into 'Christology', which looks at the first question, and 'soteriology', which looks at the second.

Christology – the study of who Jesus is in relation to God.

But actually, of course, the two questions are inextricably related. Jesus can only do what we say he does for us if he is who we say he is. The minute we go beyond the incontrovertible historical facts that a man called Jesus existed in first-century Palestine and that he inspired a group of people who continued to make converts after his death, we are into theological claims about Jesus. And even that bald historical statement begs the question 'why?'. Why did this particular man have such an effect, so that two thousand years later we are still bound to discuss him? Who was he? And who is he today?

Soteriology – the study of how God works to save us through Jesus Christ.

Cultural shifts

As we shall see, there have been a number of pivotal times in history where ways of talking about Jesus have changed and developed. These have often come as Christians try to interpret Christ to others, using languages, images and ideas that are presented by other cultures and religions.

Every one of these interpretations involves both a loss and a gain. There is always a sense of fear that the new image or translation loses something of the original, but also a sense of triumph that it can make sense in such different contexts. In the twenty-first century, it is perhaps particularly important to know that all previous Christian generations have taken risks in transmitting what they believed about Jesus. Ours is by no means the first generation to try to explain him to people of no faith or another faith. Ours is by no means the first generation to fear that we are losing the essential truths about Jesus as we attempt to make him relevant to an uncomprehending culture. But also ours is not the first generation to realize that, as we try to speak about Jesus in new language and to new people, we find he is already there. We find our own understanding challenged and enlarged by the language and images we are forced to use in order to speak of Jesus to our own culture.

That is not to say that truth is all relative. It is not to say that any way of describing Jesus is just as good as any other 'if it works for you'. Part of what we are looking at as we study these pivotal moments in Christian history are the discarded ideas. Sometimes people hold up an image or a phrase that they think will help people to see Jesus, and the rest of the Christian world says, 'No'. 'No', that does not make sense. 'No', that leaves out too much. 'No', that is a distortion. Jesus is not just a cipher for all human religious aspirations.

We say that Jesus is both completely human and completely God. Since he is the only being of whom this can be said, it is not surprising that he defies description. To provide a genuine picture of Jesus, God and man, is beyond our image-making power. But that doesn't mean we shouldn't try.

The key questions we will explore are:

- Who does Jesus have to be in order to do what he does for us? If we want to say that he 'saves' us, do we also have to say that he is both fully God and fully human?
- How can we speak about Jesus both truthfully and illuminatingly in changing circumstances? If we use new words and pictures about Jesus, how do we know that we are still talking about the same person?
- What is it that we need Jesus to do for us? What does Jesus 'save' us from or for?

Exercise

How would you describe Jesus if you were to meet someone who had never heard of him?

When you've discussed that, see if your description was mostly about who Jesus *is* or what he *does*.

1

Who Jesus Is

Finding the right words

The people who met Jesus and became his first disciples were Jews. They naturally thought of Jesus and his mission in terms of the great images and figures of their religious tradition. The Gospels suggest that Jesus was a bit wary about these identifications, and particularly of the word 'Messiah' (cf. Mark 8.29–30). It seems that the only title he used of himself was the much more ambiguous one 'Son of Man' (cf. Matthew 26.64). There might be all kinds of reasons for this hesitation – perhaps Jesus did not want to encourage his followers to believe that he had come as a political revolutionary, or perhaps none of the possible titles seemed to fit his own understanding of what God wanted him to do.

Messiah – a term taken from Jewish teaching that God would send someone to free his people and bring them back to God.

But if he didn't encourage verbal pigeon-holing by his followers, his actions were not at all ambiguous. He acted as one who had the right to speak and act for God, for example in the forgiveness of sins, or in giving judgement. Look, for example, at Mark 2.1–12, which is the story of the healing of a paralyzed man. Jesus is accused of blasphemy when he forgives the man's sins. 'Who can forgive sins but God alone?' his accusers ask. And how right they are. Or think of the cleansing of the Temple (see Matthew 21.12–13, Mark 11.15–17, Luke 19.45–6), where Jesus assumes he has the right to act on God's behalf against the mercenary practices in the Temple.

Incarnation – used to describe how God takes on human nature in Jesus. It literally means 'entering into the body'.

Wherever Jesus went, he presumed that God's presence went with him, and God's rule was supreme. In other words, where Jesus was, there the Kingship, the Kingdom of God was. This was not because he demanded worship and reverence for himself. Quite the contrary. But he did insist that in his presence, people could not pretend that God was not real. They could not go on living their lives as though God did not exist or made no claims upon them.

When the first disciples begin to preach, after Jesus' death and resurrection, they do not simply talk about him as a great teacher. They do not try to spread his 'system'. Instead, they claim that Jesus has acted for God and continues to do so, and that the only way to live in the world is the way of Jesus. But although they all agree about the centrality and continuing presence of Jesus, that doesn't mean that their ways of describing who Jesus is and what he does are the same.

Resurrection – Jesus' return from death.

Look at the different emphasis in these three passages of scripture.

Acts 2.22–36

'You that are Israelites, listen to what I have to say: Jesus of Nazareth, a man attested to you by God with deeds of power, wonders, and signs that God did through him among you, as you yourselves know – this man, handed over to you according to the definite plan and foreknowledge of God, you crucified and killed by the hands of those outside the law. But God raised him up, having freed him from death, because it was impossible for him to be held in its power. For David says concerning him,

"I saw the Lord always before me, for he is at my right hand so that I will not be shaken; therefore my heart was glad, and my tongue rejoiced; moreover, my flesh will live in hope. For you will not abandon my soul to Hades, or let your Holy One experience corruption. You have made known to me the ways of life; you will make me full of gladness with your presence."

'Fellow Israelites, I may say to you confidently of our ancestor David that he both died and was buried, and his tome is with us to this day. Since he was a prophet, he knew that God had sworn with an oath to him that he would put one of his descendants on his throne. Foreseeing this, David spoke of the resurrection of the Messiah, saying,

"He was not abandoned to Hades, nor did his flesh experience corruption."

This Jesus God raised up, and of that all of us are witnesses. Being therefore exalted at the right hand of God, and having received from the Father the promise of the Holy Spirit, he has poured out this that you both see and hear. For David did not ascend into the heavens, but he himself says,

"The Lord said to my Lord, 'Sit at my right hand, until I make your enemies your footstool.'"

Therefore let the entire house of Israel know with certainty that God has made him both Lord and Messiah, this Jesus whom you crucified.'

Peter's speech in Acts is clearly aimed at a Jewish audience, whose first question is about how Jesus relates to the Jewish God and the Jewish scriptures. They seem to be people who had heard of Jesus, but who had assumed that his death was all the proof necessary that he was not acting for God. So the speech has to demonstrate how suffering and Messiahship are not incompatible, and how anyone who truly reads the scriptures ought to be able to see the match between God's activity in the nation's past and his activity in Jesus.

Notice the Jewish context:

- Emphasis on the fulfilment of Jewish scriptures.
- Claims that Jesus is greater than David.
- Jesus is the promised Messiah.

Notice the references to what the audience might already know about the human historical Jesus:

- He was a wonder worker.
- He was crucified.

What does the passage claim that Jesus does for us?
The main emphasis, for this audience, seems to be on who Jesus is.

1 Corinthians 15.1–8

'Now I should remind you, brothers and sisters, of the good news that I proclaimed to you, which you in turn received, in which also you stand, through which also you are being saved, if you hold firmly to the message that I proclaimed to you – unless you have come to believe in vain.

'For I handed on to you as of first importance what I in turn had received: that Christ died for our sins in accordance with the scriptures, and that he was buried, and that he was raised on the third day in accordance with the scriptures, and that he appeared to Cephas, then to the twelve. Then he appeared to more than five hundred brothers and sisters at one time, most of whom are still alive, though some have died. Then he appeared to James, then to all the apostles. Last of all, as to someone untimely born, he appeared also to me.'

Notice that there is already a 'tradition' that is handed down about Jesus. It includes:

- His death and resurrection.

- The claim that his death and resurrection are the fulfilment of Jewish scriptures.
- That his resurrection is testified to by a number of different sources.
- That his death is 'for our sins' – without any further explanation, as though this would be well known to Paul's readers.

This passage has less to say about who Jesus is and is more interested in what he does for us. The references to the historical Jesus are limited to his death and resurrection.

1 Peter 2.21–25

'For to this you have been called, because Christ also suffered for you, leaving you an example, so that you should follow in his steps.
   "He committed no sin, and no deceit was found in his mouth."
   'When he was abused, he did not return abuse; when he suffered, he did not threaten; but he entrusted himself to the one who judges justly. He himself bore our sins in his body on the cross, so that, free from sins, we might live for righteousness; by his wounds you have been healed. For you were going astray like sheep, but now you have returned to the shepherd and guardian of your souls.'

Notice again the emphasis on the purpose of Jesus' sufferings – for our sins.
The main point of this passage is as an encouragement to discipleship in the face of suffering – we are to imitate Christ.

From Messiah to Logos

The earliest Christians thought that Jesus would only really make sense to Jews. They expected Jesus' followers to remain within Judaism, changing it no doubt, as they gradually persuaded their co-religionists to read the Jewish scriptures with the new interpretative key they were providing. But very early in the life of the new sect, they are forced to think about whether they are to stick to their Jewish roots or not. People who are not Jewish come to them, longing to hear about Jesus. Acts and the letters of Paul show what a struggle it was for those first Christians to decide whether they could faithfully preach Jesus to a non-Jewish audience without asking them to become Jews, or whether they would be betraying their understanding of Jesus if they did. The first two chapters of Galatians show how much conflict the issue generated, and how hard Paul had to fight to get his 'gospel for the uncircumcised' (Galatians 2.7) recognized. Paul preaches Jesus with an impassioned certainty that Jesus is of universal significance. Jesus' saving work is not limited to one set of people, and so it can and must be described in many different ways.

Creed – coming from the Latin word 'credo', meaning 'I believe', a creed is an agreed statement of faith.

The first chapter of John's Gospel represents an expression of who Jesus is for the whole world. It says, for example, 'All things came into being through him, and without him not one thing came into being' (John 1.3).

Logos – Greek for 'Word'. It is widely used as a name for Christ, and emphasizes that Christ is the way that God 'communicates' with the world.

It isn't necessary to have grown up with the Jewish scriptures or the idea of the coming Messiah in order to understand what John is claiming about Jesus. The language that John uses when he calls Jesus 'the Word' or *Logos* would have been familiar to most literate people in his Greek-speaking society, whatever their religious background. John's is a culture that is used to discussion of divine activity. It is particularly interested in the question of how we can know the inexpressible and unknowable divine being, and how God, who is perfect, whole and not dependent on anything else, can give rise to a world that is outside God. Most of the sophisticated religious philosophers of the day would have spoken of ways in which the unknowable and unchangeable divine essence can be mediated to the imperfect and changing world. Jewish philosophers, for example, spoke of Wisdom as the outgoing creative aspect of God. If you look at Proverbs 8, you will see a description of Wisdom as almost personified:

'The Lord created me at the beginning of his work,' Wisdom says, 'and I was daily his delight rejoicing before him always.'

Proverbs 8. 22, 30

Christians picked up on this language very quickly as a way of helping to explain what they were saying about Jesus. Jesus is the one through whom we come to know God. He is the outgoing, seeking, creative love of God, which makes us and redeems us. 'Wisdom' and 'Logos' are word-pictures that are already around in the culture, and Christians use them very effectively.

But as they use them, they also change them. Most Jews reading Proverbs 8 would assume that this was a metaphor, while most Christians reading it would assume it was a description of an actual being – Jesus. The language also has dangers. Although it says a lot about the power of this mediator-figure and his closeness to God, it does also imply that the mediator is subordinate to God, and may have been made by God for this particular role, rather than being, properly speaking, divine himself.

From 'like God' to God

This ambiguity caused another of the great shifts in the traditional description of Jesus. In the fourth century a teacher and preacher called Arius thought he would help to resolve the uncertainties inherent in 'Logos/ Word' language by coming down on one side. Jesus is not 'God', Arius argued. Instead, he is an infinitely superior created being, whose job it is to make the connection between our world and the divine sphere. Without the Logos, we could not begin to know God.

Arius held up this description of Jesus, which he believed faithfully expressed what was inherent in the tradition he had inherited. But the rest of the Christian world said 'No'. They did not say it unanimously and at once. It took over a century of fierce verbal and sometimes physical fighting before Arius' clarifying description of Jesus was finally rejected. But in the end what won the day was the insistence that Jesus cannot do what he does for us if he is not God. If he is basically tied up in the human situation, as we are, without any extra resources, then what good can he do us? He has to be able to bring God's creative power into our human situation, and to do that, he has to be on both sides of the equation at once. He has to be both God and human.

From pilgrims to civil servants

At the point in the fourth century when Arius was trying to straighten out the description of Jesus, there was also another factor that led to greater pressure for clarity, and that was the involvement of a Christian emperor. The emperor Constantine became a Christian after, as he believed, the cross of Christ brought him a decisive victory in battle. And suddenly, being a Christian became respectable. What's more, disputes between Christians became public issues in a way that would have been unimaginable when Paul and Peter were arguing about whether or not converts had to be circumcised.

Homoousios – 'of one being'. The Greek word used to resolve the fourth-century debate about how Jesus relates to God.

The emperor called together Christian representatives from all over his empire to discuss, among other things, the question raised by Arius' teaching. The Council of Nicaea decisively rejected Arius' definition of Jesus in favour of one that says that Jesus is 'of the same being' as God. This is the word still used in Christian creeds today. In Greek, it is the word 'homoousios', and it is variously translated as 'of one being' or 'of one substance'. What it means is that whatever God is, Jesus Christ is too. The council did not settle the matter completely, partly because the word 'homoousios', which had been employed to get rid of one set of ambiguities about the nature of Christ, introduced other questions in its place. Some people thought it meant that Christ is 'very like' God, while others thought it meant that Christ was just an aspect of God, and not in any way distinguishable from the Father. It took another century before the description of Christ as both fully human and fully God became the norm, and even then some Christians did not like the image and were not sure that it really represented what they wanted to say about Jesus.

So part of the price paid for public acceptance and for clearer definitions was division. The minute you start saying that one description of Jesus is normative, there are some who feel that their own understanding has been rejected. And with the weight of the emperor behind the central definition, contrasting images cannot co-exist. They have to separate. There has been both a gain and a loss. A gain in precision and clarity and a loss of the tolerance that ambiguity might allow.

From 'Jesus' to 'Christ'

One of the unforeseeable consequences of the defining process of the first few Christian centuries is the gradual obscuring of the human, historical Jesus in favour of the more abstract 'Christ' or 'Logos'. The strange, dynamic, authoritative Jesus of the gospels, who confronts people with the demands of God, and who forgives their sins and heals them was still read and preached, of course, but his image was overlaid in public discourse and public art with the Christ in majesty, whose authority is symbolized by his imperial robes. His power of forgiveness and his ability to bring people into the presence of God becomes institutionalized and ritualized in the structures and ceremonies of the church. Once again, this is both loss and gain. The universality of places and practices where people can meet God in Christ might well make up for the lack of focus on Jesus himself.

Christ – the Greek word for 'Messiah' – the person God was expected to send to save his people. It has become a proper name for Jesus, and is often used to distinguish the historical human Jesus from the divine Christ, the second person of the Trinity.

But Christian prayer and devotion in every age constantly rediscovers the 'real' Jesus. Mystics like Julian of Norwich encounter him in the bitterness of his death and are entranced by the love that led to the cross. Luther, the faithful monk, rediscovers him as the one who brings freedom from fear of God's judgement. Martyrs like Janani Luwum, an Archbishop of Uganda, rediscover him as the victim whose powerlessness brings victory. In the centuries between Constantine and the modern world, the balance between institutional definitions of Jesus and personal images of him shifts backwards and forwards. Arguably, the Reformation is a movement to reclaim the right of every believer to discover Jesus afresh, rather than just to accept the definitions offered by the church.

But underlying all of these pictures, waiting to be given form and colour by the pictures being made, is the vital if abstract material of the claim now made about Jesus. He is both God and human. If he is to bring into our situation something that we cannot provide ourselves, he must be God. If he is to do that in a way that is of any use to us, he has to be human.

Summary

In order to bring God's creativity into the real situation we human beings actually live in, Christian tradition claims that Jesus must be both fully human and fully God.

Exercise

1 The process we have just been looking at in this section involves lots of different kinds of images, taken from the cultures in which the debate about Jesus was going on (e.g. Messiah, *Logos*, *homoousios*, etc.). Are there images and words from our own culture that you think are particularly appropriate to help to communicate Jesus to our world?

2 Have you ever been 'turned off' or felt alienated from Jesus by someone or some group's description of him? If so, try to analyze why.

2

What Jesus Does

We have already suggested that, if Jesus is to do for us what Christians claim that he does, he has to be fully human and fully God. That also gives us clues about what it is that we think we need God to do for us. Clearly, it is something that we cannot do for ourselves. The effect of the coming of Jesus is to bring into our human situation something that was not there before. But how is this best described?

Jesus pays the price

> Christ . . . entered once for all into the Holy Place, not with the blood of goats and calves, but with his own blood, thus obtaining eternal redemption.
>
> *Hebrews 9.12*

One of the standard ways in which the work of Jesus is described is in sacrificial language. To the first Christians, used to the Jewish Temple system, where actual sacrifices were made, this clearly made sense. But even without such a system, the language of sacrifice still resonates. We speak of soldiers sacrificing their lives to save their countries. We speak of parents sacrificing themselves for their children. We know that the Jewish Christian nun, Edith Stein, took the place of another in the Nazi gas chambers, so giving her own life to save someone else's.

The great strength of this language is that it emphasizes the cost. It is no light and easy thing that God does for us. It costs Jesus his life. It is the cross of Jesus Christ that buys our release from bondage, and only Jesus, who is both human and divine, can make a sacrifice that is worth enough to do it. Only his death can pay the price.

But the drawback with this idea is that we can't help wondering who is demanding this sacrifice. Is it God the Father? If so, isn't it rather mean of him? Could he not just agree freely to wipe out our debt? We admit that we have done all kinds of things wrong, and might well owe God a lot, but surely he does not really need a death to satisfy him? So perhaps it is the devil who demands this price? Perhaps our actions have put us deeply in debt to the devil, and Jesus has to pay our ransom with his life? But that suggests that the devil is the equal of God and can demand things from him.

So although this language has emotional power, it is probably not enough on its own.

Jesus the victor

> And when you were dead in trespasses and the uncircumcision of your flesh, God made you alive together with him, when he forgave us all our trespasses, erasing the record that stood against us with its legal demands. He set this aside, nailing it to the cross. He disarmed the rulers and authorities and made a public example of them, triumphing over them in it.'
>
> *Colossians 2.13–15*

Similar kinds of strengths and weaknesses go with the idea that Jesus wins a victory in order to set us free. This language emphasizes the fact that something decisive has happened. Thanks to the work of God in Jesus Christ, we are now in a different situation. The war is won. But whom was Jesus fighting on our behalf? And why was his death necessary? What kind of a victory is it that we are talking about?

Jesus the guru

> For to this you have been called, because Christ also suffered for you, leaving you an example, so that you should follow in his steps.
>
> *1 Peter 2.21*

Both of these ways of describing what Jesus does for us, either as the one who pays the price or as the one who wins the victory, make it clear that we are utterly dependent upon the initiative of God to do for us what we could not do for ourselves. But they do not make it clear how we should now live. If God has done for us everything that needs doing to bring about our salvation, why are we not better people? Why is the world not transformed, if the price has been paid and the victory won? Doesn't the fact that we continue to sin suggest that there is yet more to be done? In fact, both these theories, as classically developed, answer these concerns, to some extent. Paul, for example, suggests that we now live our lives in grateful response to what God has done. We live as though Jesus' death puts to death our old way of life, so that we can now start again (see Romans 6.1–4, to see what I am paraphrasing).

But that can still make us sound very passive, so some theories about what it is that Jesus does for us prefer to put the ball squarely back in our court. Jesus sets us the example of how we should live. His wise teaching and his parables give us advice and insight into God and the world. He shows us the perfect human life, living in obedience to God and so free from sin, and it is now up to us to try to follow that example. If we all try to live like Jesus, the world will indeed be transformed.

The major problem with this is that we seem sadly unable to follow Jesus' great example. And this fact is also a problem for our next theory.

Jesus the liberator

So you are no longer a slave but a child, and if a child then also an heir, through God.

Galatians 4.7

Liberation theology – one modern rediscovery of what Jesus does for us, based on a re-reading of the Gospels. The Jesus we meet in the Gospels noticeably addresses his message not to the well-off and the pious, but to the poor and the needy and those who know they are in need of God. In the centuries that followed, as Christianity became respectable and powerful and wealthy, this aspect of Jesus' message was sometimes lost. 'Salvation' then all too easily becomes something that happens only after death, without having any great effect on people's present situation, which may be fine for those who live in comfort now.

But Jesus was not content to leave people in a state of pious acceptance of their fate, liberation theologians argue. Instead, he preached 'the Kingdom of God', a time when the world-order will change so dramatically that all human hierarchies and institutions will respond directly to God. And Jesus seemed to think that in his own ministry people were already encountering the Kingdom of God, through his teaching, his healing and his presence with them. Jesus expected to change people's lives dramatically, just as dramatically as God did when he brought his people out of slavery in Egypt and into the freedom of the promised Land. That was no theoretical salvation, and neither is the salvation that Jesus brings about.

What Jesus does for us, then, according to Liberation theology, is to fire us with a longing for a world that truly reflects God's priorities of justice and equitable community for all. In our lives together as Christians we have a glimpse of what God longs to give to all the world, and so we are motivated to fight against sin, which is all the structures and instincts in the world that militate against justice.

This is Jon Sobrino's discussion of what the Resurrection of Jesus means:

Preaching the resurrection-event itself is not the only action or work of service set in motion by Jesus' resurrection. We must also serve the reality for which we are allowed to hope by virtue of his resurrection. We cannot preach the resurrection of Jesus if we do not have the active *intention* to flesh out in reality the hope that finds expression there . . .

In the last analysis the resurrection sets in motion a life of service designed to implement in reality the eschatological ideals of justice, peace and human solidarity. It is the earnest attempt to make those ideals *real* that enables us to comprehend what happened in Jesus' resurrection.

In general we can say that the resurrection is laid hold of not only in hopeful expectation for the end of history but in here-and-now love.

Christology at the Crossroads, SCM 1978, pp. 254–5

This basic insight of Liberation theology – that Jesus comes fundamentally to change the world, and to inspire us to join him – is picked up in other forms of theology that challenge cultural norms. So, for example, Black theology and Feminist theology call for us to be inspired and empowered by Jesus in order to overcome elitist practices, based on white male privilege. They point out that Jesus implicitly critiques all normal models of power. Although he is God incarnate, he chooses not to force his will on people, but to suffer and die. If that is the creative power of God at work in our world, then systems that enshrine and privilege the power of one group over another must be called into question.

In all these theologies, what Jesus does for us is primarily to inspire, and it is not clear that he *has* to be fully God in order to do this, though the critique of prevailing norms becomes more pointed and pressing if they are assumed to be contrary to the nature of God, as we meet him in Jesus.

Jesus the doctor

Those who are well have no need of a physician, but those who are sick; I have come to call not the righteous but sinners.

Mark 2.17

Healing metaphors might be another potential way of talking about what Jesus does for us. They combine some of the powerful sense of something being *achieved*, something being *different* because of what Jesus does for us, which is the great strength of models of victory or paying the price. To speak of Jesus as the one who heals our sickness also takes seriously our own involvement in the process of transformation, as do liberation and moral example models. We need to co-operate with our own healing, and do the exercises that our healer has set us, exercises of prayer and grace and living together. We could even extend the healing metaphor into an illuminating way of speaking about the role of the Christian church. Perhaps we could imagine that, thanks to the blood transfusion Jesus gives us, we now carry the antibodies that can provide healing for the world.

This kind of language takes seriously the biblical description of our state before the coming of Christ. We are so ill that we must die. Only Jesus can save us.

The most powerful modern expositions of Jesus as the great healer have come from looking at the relationship between human beings and God in what happens at the crucifixion. Jesus is crucified because of all the aggression and hatred and fear that he evokes in people as he confronts them with God. The only way we can cope with Jesus' challenge to us is to get rid of him. The cross looks like the ultimate triumph of human power, and Jesus appears powerless to prevent it. He simply suffers the fury and the pain inflicted upon him, without any attempt at retaliation. But in doing this he creates a space. He absorbs all the wild negative emotion thrown at him and stops it, holds it. Because he refuses to give back like violence for like, his powerlessness actually becomes a source of life-giving power. We have nothing further, more dreadful that we can think of to do to him, because we thought we had already done the worst, in killing him, but it wasn't enough. Jesus absorbs our sin and gives it back to us as life.

Summary and conclusions

In his classic book on the Atonement, *Christus Victor*, the Swedish theologian Gustav Aulen divided theories of the Atonement into three groups.

- The first, which Aulen himself thought was the best, are theories that cluster around the idea of victory. Jesus triumphs over evil and so frees the human race from bondage.
- The second, which Aulen called the 'Latin' type, has the legal motif as its controlling image. An offence has been committed against God's holy honour by human sinfulness, and the proper compensation must be paid to release us from prison. In his death, Jesus pays that price for us, takes our place and satisfies God.
- The third group of theories are basically about reconciliation. We are

alienated from God by our sinfulness, and Jesus comes to reconcile us to God again. These theories can be just about Jesus' good example, or they can imply, more strongly, that Jesus reunites us by holding human and divine nature together in himself and in his death.

All of these groups of theories have some biblical foundation, and all have been used by Christians to explain what we believe Jesus does for us in his life, death and resurrection.

> *Atonement* – the forgiveness of our sin, leading to our reconciliation with God, through the death of Jesus Christ.

Perhaps what is needed is some kind of combination of all of these theories, if that is possible. We need the insight of Jesus as the one who pays the price or wins the victory to show that God acts decisively in ways that we are not capable of, and objectively changes the state of the relationship between himself and us. 'Sin' is whatever it is that has separated us from God, and made us incapable of living with him as we are supposed to, and that is what God comes to tackle, in Jesus. Both we and our world have been deeply damaged by our attempts to live as though we were not made to live with God, and so God's way of reconnecting with us is very costly. God does not just wave a magic wand and unmake everything we have done, including us ourselves. Instead, he works with what we have done, and takes it into himself, so that nothing can now separate us from the love of God in Christ. Even sin and death are now forced, through the sheer vitality and creativity of the life of God now running through them, to submit to God. They no longer have the power to create a barrier between God and us.

That does not immediately change our nature. It is like when the Israelites are freed from slavery in Egypt. Objectively, they are now free, but if you read about them as they wander in the wilderness, it is clear that, mentally, they are still slaves. They have transferred their feelings of dependence and anger to Moses. They do not expect to have to take responsibility for themselves.

So we can work with the knowledge that God has freed us and, at the same time, add elements from the images of Jesus as guru, liberator and doctor. Jesus is an example to us, and we are expected to see his transforming and liberating work and to try to join in with it. We are now free people, and nothing can force us back into slavery. But now, in response to what God has done, we can try to live like God's children, partners in his enterprise. We will continue to make mistakes, but that will not take away our freedom to relate to God. Through our willingness to emulate Jesus, we can become transformative people, too. We, too, to some extent at least, can accept the aggression and anger that is thrown at us by those who still think they are slaves, and we can refuse to return hatred for hatred. That way, we too can begin to change the psychology of the world.

These are large claims that Christians make about Jesus. And while most people of other faiths and no faith would agree that Jesus is worthy of honour and respect, they do not agree that Jesus is fully human and fully divine and that his death is the way to reconciliation with God. It is a bitter irony that as Christians we have sometimes used our fundamental belief that 'God was in Christ reconciling the world to himself' as a weapon to divide us from each other, thereby, presumably, making God's reconciling work even harder. If God does really reach out to his people through Jesus, coming to share our lives before we ask or even know our need, let alone before we begin to understand, then it does seem clear that it ought to be the duty of Christ's followers to be reconcilers, too.

In the end, all the complex and technical statements that Christians need to make to explain the love of God in Christ come back to this primary experience – that we are called on to worship Jesus Christ with gratitude and praise, and to be his disciples, his followers, in all we do.

Exercise

1 Do you find one of the above images more helpful than the others? Would you like to add any more?
2 What would you say that Jesus has done for you?

3

Case Studies

1 'The intelligence of the victim'

In a remarkable book, *The Joy of Being Wrong*, James Alison explores the idea that Jesus, in his life, death and resurrection, makes possible a radical restructuring of what it is to be human. He deliberately allows himself to be made a victim so as to reveal the true nature of God and of human beings:

> What we have then is a gradual process of the recasting of God in the light of the resurrection of Jesus, so that it is seen that the previous discourse, within which Jesus had operated and within which his victimary self-understanding was forged, was in fact a provisional discourse. In the light of the resurrection it gradually becomes possible to see that it was not that God was previously violent, now blessing now cursing (see Deuteronomy 32.39), but had now brought all that ambivalence to an end. Rather it became possible to see that that was all human violence, with various degrees of projection on to God. God had been from the beginning always, immutably, love, and this love was made manifest in sending God's Son into the midst of violent humans, even into the midst of their persecutory projections of God, so that they might treat him as a human victim and thus reveal the depth of the love of God, who was prepared to be a human victim simultaneously to show the depth of his love for humanity and to reveal humanity as having been locked into the realm of the Father of lies.
>
> *p. 108*

Humans are always moved by another. Either it is the other of pacific self-donation, or the other which maintains order by expulsion and killing. Knowing the Father is being a human who tends towards the victim; not knowing the Father is being a human who lives by creating victims.

p. 110

Exercise

1 Do you recognize these descriptions of the only two ways of being human – either caring for victims or creating victims?
2 How do the life, death and resurrection of Jesus change the human understanding of God?
3 What do you think is missing from this account of the work of God in Christ Jesus?

2 Knowing Jesus as our Saviour

The German theologian, Jurgen Moltmann, has suggested that the central Christian creeds often fail to remind us of who it is we are actually talking about. The claims made about Jesus are based on what he said and did, and Moltmann suggests adding some of those things to our usual recital:

> Baptised by John the Baptist
> filled with the Holy Spirit
> to preach the kingdom of God to the poor
> to heal the sick
> to receive those who have been cast out,
> to revive Israel for the salvation of the nations, and
> to have mercy upon all people.

J. Moltmann, *The Way of Jesus Christ*, p. 149

Exercise

1 Why do you think Moltmann has chosen these particular characteristics of Jesus' life as necessary to our understanding of who Jesus is and what he does for us?
2 On the basis of your own reading of the Bible, what other elements would you add as necessary for a proper description of Jesus?

3 Deep magic

In *The Lion, the Witch and the Wardrobe*, C. S. Lewis describes a fictional world called Narnia, which four children visit, by magic. One of the four, Edmund, betrays the others to the White Witch and falls into her power himself. He then has to be saved by the great Lion, Aslan, who is Narnia's Jesus-figure. The White Witch agrees to free Edmund provided that Aslan pays the price that the 'deep magic from the dawn of time' decrees is her right. So Aslan allows himself to be put to death in Edmund's place. But his resurrection shows that there is still deeper magic built into the world.

'It means', said Aslan, 'that though the Witch knew the Deep Magic, there is a magic deeper still which she did not know. Her knowledge goes back only to the dawn of time. But if she could have looked a little further back, into the stillness and the darkness before Time dawned, she would have read there a different incantation. She would have known that when a willing victim who had committed no treachery was killed in a traitor's stead, the Table would crack and Death itself would start working backwards.'

Exercise

1 This is clearly Lewis's way of making vivid a particular understanding of the Atonement. What are the strengths and weaknesses of Lewis's analogy?
2 Lewis tackles, head on, all the images of Jesus' death as 'paying the price in our place'. These are often thought of as the controlling nexus of descriptions of what Jesus does for us on the cross. Are they the most important elements of your own understanding of the work of Jesus?
3 What other fictional or poetic writing have you found helpful in thinking about the death of Jesus?

Further Resources

So much has been written about Jesus that it is hard to know where to start!

Hymnbooks

You might like to have a look at hymnbooks or songbooks used in your local church and see what some of the writers say about Jesus. Because songs have to be reasonably simple, singable and devotional, they often express theological statements quite clearly.

Books

James Alison, 1998, *The Joy of Being Wrong*, Crossroads.
Church of England Doctrine Commission Report, 1995, *The Mystery of Salvation*, Church House Publishing.
Gustav Aulen, 1931, *Christus Victor*, London.
Paul Fiddes, 1989, *Past Event and Present Salvation*, Darton Longman and Todd.
Colin Gunton, 1988, *The Actuality of Atonement*, T and T Clark.
Sebastian Moore, 1977, *The Crucified is No Stranger*, New York.
Stephen Sykes, 1997, *The Story of Atonement*, Darton Longman and Todd.
N. T. Wright, 1992, *Who Was Jesus?* SPCK.

Websites

If you type in 'Jesus Christ' you come up with so many possible sites that it is positively bewildering. Most of them are conservative, American and concerned to give you 'answers' to the questions you are supposed to ask. They can be quite helpful, nonetheless.